WITHDRAWN

W9-BIC-355

Exploring the Seasons
Exploring Winter

by Terri DeGezelle

CAPSTONE PRESS
a capstone imprint

Pebble Plus is published by Capstone Press,
1710 Roe Crest Drive, North Mankato, Minnesota 56003.
www.capstonepub.com

Copyright © 2012 by Capstone Press, a Capstone imprint. All rights reserved.
No part of this publication may be reproduced in whole or in part, or stored in a retrieval system, or transmitted in any
form or by any means, electronic, mechanical, photocopying, recording, or otherwise, without written permission of the
publisher. For information regarding permission, write to Capstone Press,
1710 Roe Crest Drive, North Mankato, Minnesota 56003.

Books published by Capstone Press are manufactured with paper
containing at least 10 percent post-consumer waste.

Library of Congress Cataloging-in-Publication Data
DeGezelle, Terri, 1955–
    Exploring winter / by Terri DeGezelle.
        p. cm. — (Pebble plus. Exploring the seasons)
    Includes bibliographical references and index.
    Summary: "Color photos and simple text introduce the winter season"—Provided by publisher.
    ISBN 978-1-4296-7699-1 (library binding) — ISBN 978-1-4296-7916-9 (paperback)
    1. Winter—Juvenile literature. I. Title. II. Series.
    QB637.8.D438 2012
    508.2—dc23   2011029894

Editorial Credits
Gillia Olson, editor; Sarah Bennett, designer; Svetlana Zhurkin, media researcher; Kathy McColley, production specialist

Photo Credits
Dreamstime: Savenkov, 10–11; iStockphoto: Linda Kloosterhof, cover (center), Ziva_K, 5; Shutterstock: Anatoliy
Nikolaevich Zavodskov, cover (right), Andromed, 14–15, Dainis Derics, 12–13, Gerald A. DeBoer, 1, Jaren Jai Wicklund,
18–19, Joe Ng, 20 (inset), Songquan Deng, 20–21; Visuals Unlimited/Stephen Lang, 16–17

Note to Parents and Teachers

The Exploring the Seasons series supports national science standards related to earth science.
This book describes and illustrates the winter season. The images support early readers in
understanding the text. The repetition of words and phrases helps early readers learn new
words. This book also introduces early readers to subject-specific vocabulary words, which are
defined in the Glossary section. Early readers may need assistance to read some words and to
use the Table of Contents, Glossary, Read More, Internet Sites, and Index sections of the book.

Printed in the United States of America in North Mankato, Minnesota.
062012   006762R

Table of Contents

Cold, Cold, Cold

Winter days are the shortest

and coldest of the year.

In the Northern Hemisphere,

the first day of the winter season

is December 21 or 22.

What Causes Seasons?

Earth spins on a tilted axis.

Earth also moves around the sun.

The tilt makes certain parts

of the planet point at the sun

at different times of the year.

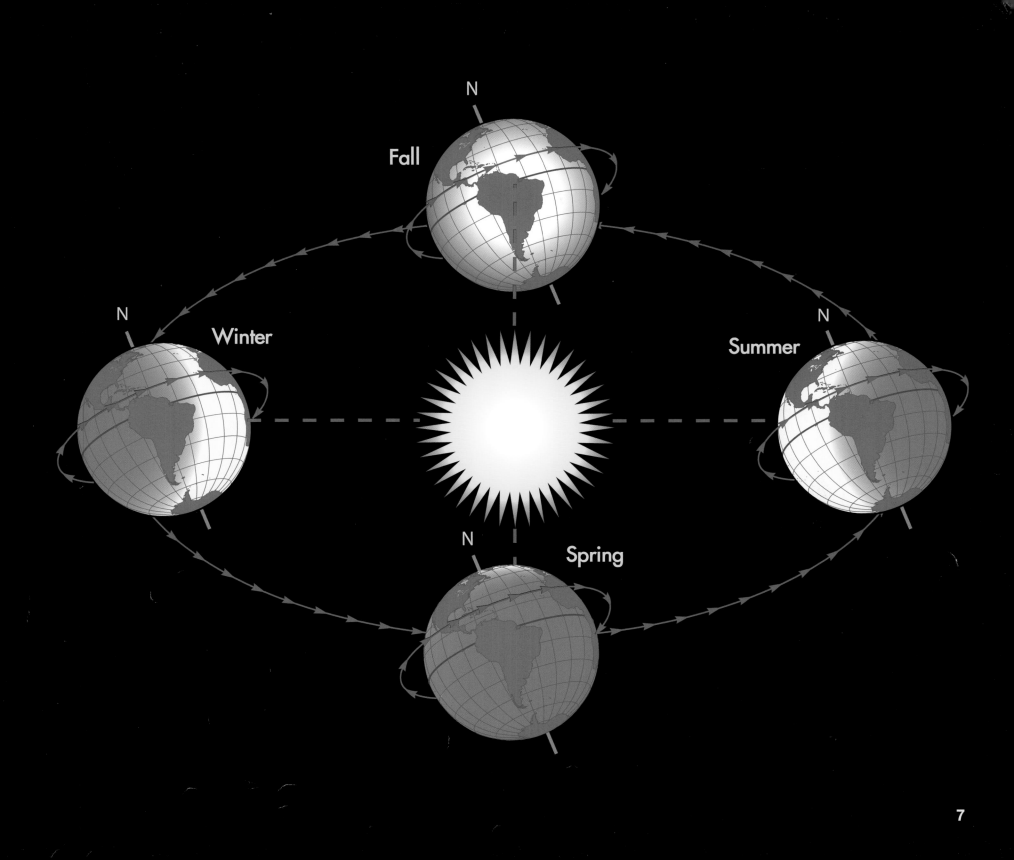

Fall

Winter

Summer

Spring

The seasons change as different parts of Earth point at the sun. Winter begins when Earth's axis points most directly away from the sun.

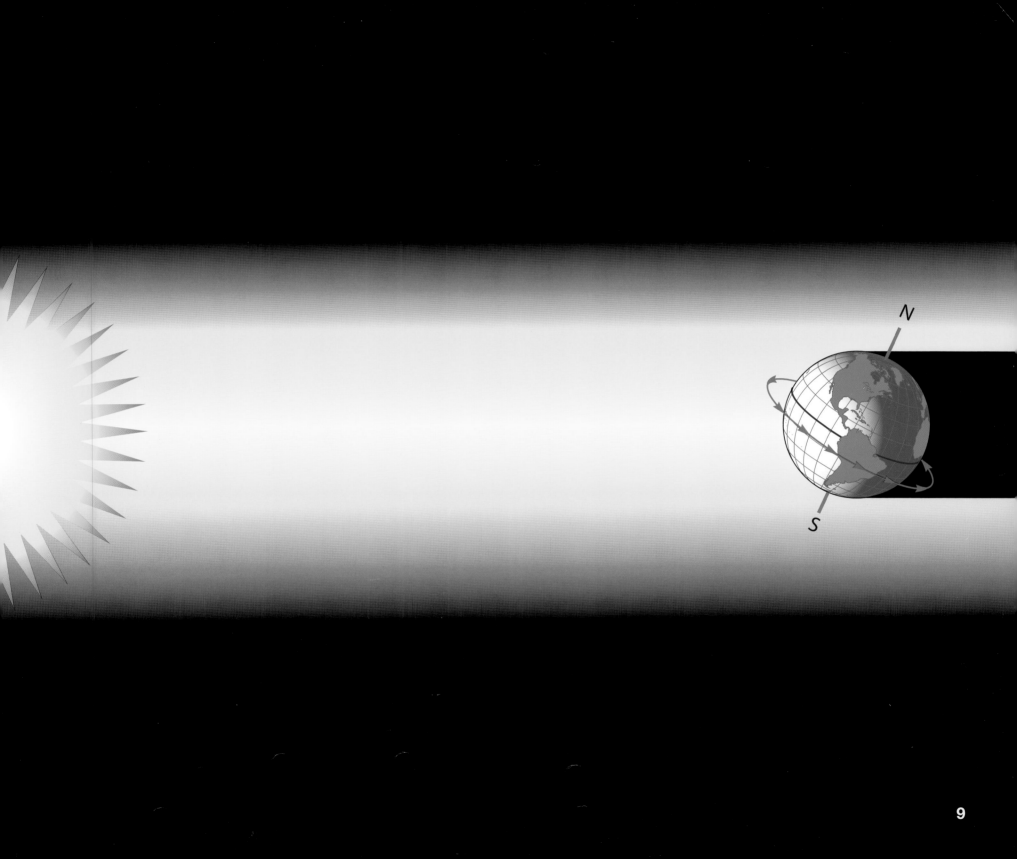

Daylight

Daylight is shortest in winter. The sun is low in the sky. Less sun makes temperatures cold. Some places get snow in winter.

Water in Winter

In colder places, lakes and ponds freeze over in winter. Snow falls instead of rain. Heavy snow and high winds can form blizzards.

Trees in Winter

Pine and spruce trees stay green in winter. Other trees may look dead, but they are dormant. They rest and wait for warmer spring weather.

Animals in Winter

Winter usually means animals can't find as much food. Squirrels eat nuts and seeds they stored in fall. Bears hibernate lightly in dens.

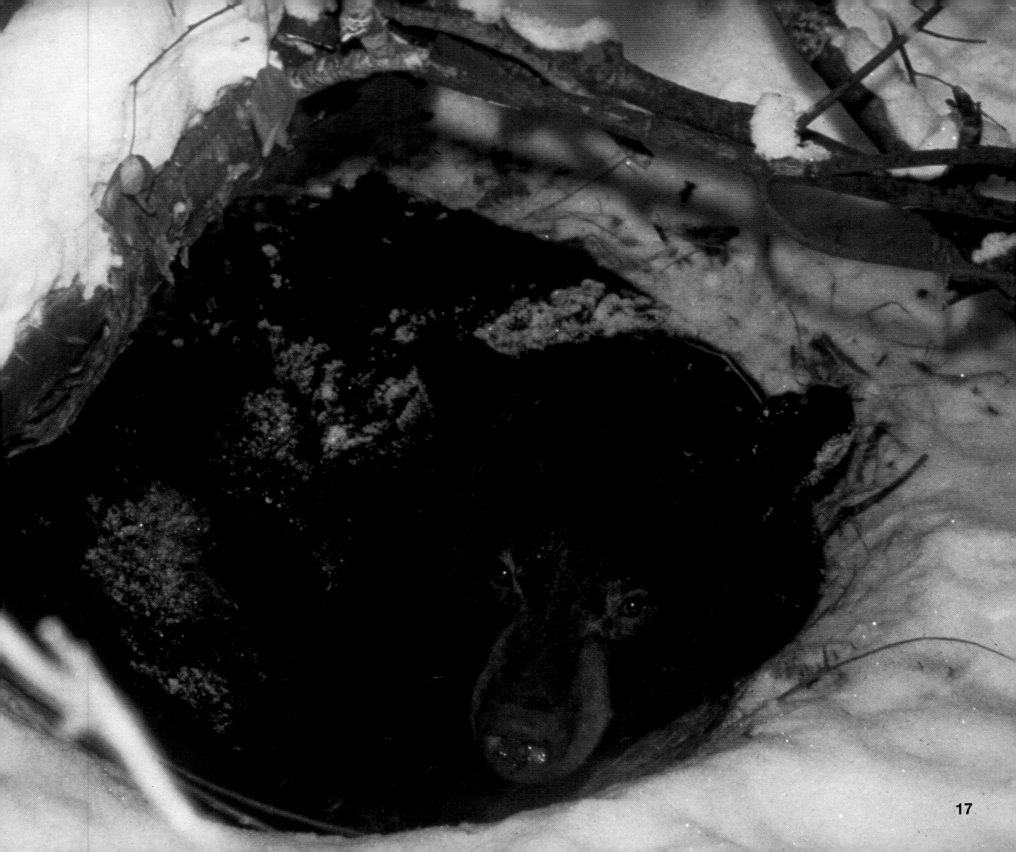

People in Winter

People dress for cold activities in winter. They wear heavy coats, hats, and boots. People sled, ski, and play in the snow.

North and South

As the Northern Hemisphere has winter, the Southern Hemisphere has summer. New Year's Day is cold in most U.S. states. But it's beach weather in Australia.

Glossary

axis—a real or imaginary line through an object's center, around which the object turns

blizzard—a heavy snowstorm with strong wind; a blizzard can last several days

dormant—not active

hemisphere—one half of Earth; the Northern and Southern hemispheres experience seasons opposite to each other

hibernate—to spend winter in a deep sleep; animals hibernate to survive low temperatures and lack of food

season—one of the four parts of the year; winter, spring, summer, and fall are seasons

temperature—how hot or cold something is

tilt—leaning; not straight

Read More

Anderson, Sheila. *Are You Ready for Winter?* Our Four Seasons. Minneapolis: Lerner Publications, 2010.

Smith, Sian. *Winter.* Seasons. Chicago: Heinemann Library, 2009.

Stewart, Melissa. *Under the Snow.* Atlanta: Peachtree, 2009.

Internet Sites

FactHound offers a safe, fun way to find Internet sites related to this book. All of the sites on FactHound have been researched by our staff.

Here's all you do:

Visit *www.facthound.com*

Type in this code: 9781429676991

Super-cool stuff! Check out projects, games and lots more at **www.capstonekids.com**

Index

Word Count: 222
Grade: 1
Early-Intervention Level: 21